READING POWER

Coming to America

Why Japanese Immigrants Came to America

Lewis K. Parker

The Rosen Publishing Group's
PowerKids Press™
New York

Published in 2003 by The Rosen Publishing Group, Inc.
29 East 21st Street, New York, NY 10010

First Edition

Book Design: Mindy Liu and Erica Clendening

Photo Credits: Cover © Kelly Mooney Photography/Corbis; pp. 4, 6, 7, 9, 11 (bottom), 16, 17, 18 Library of Congress, Prints and Photographs Division; p. 5 © MapArt; pp. 11 (top), 15 © Corbis; pp. 12–13 courtesy Gardena City Clerk's Office; p. 19 © The Mariners' Museum/Corbis; p. 20 © AP/Wide World Photos; p. 21 (top) courtesy Gilroy Historical Museum; p. 21 (bottom) © Michael S. Yamashita/Corbis

Library of Congress Cataloging-in-Publication Data

Parker, Lewis K.
Why Japanese immigrants came to America / Lewis K. Parker.
 p. cm. — (Coming to America)
Summary: Explores Japanese immigration to the United States from the 1880s to the present, and looks at the contributions of Japanese Americans to the culture of the United States.
Includes bibliographical references and index.
ISBN 0-8239-6463-9 (lib. bdg.)
1. Japanese American—History—Juvenile literature. 2. Immigrants—United States—History—Juvenile literature. 3. United States—Emigration and immigration—History—Juvenile literature. 4. Japan—Emigration and immigration—History—Juvenile literature. [1. Japanese Americans—History. 2. Immigrants—History. 3. United States—Emigration and immigration. 4. Japan—Emigration and immigration.] I. Title.
E184.J3 P37 2003
973'.04956—dc21

                                    2002002930

Contents

Trading with Japan

For hundreds of years, Japan had very little to do with other countries in the world. However, in 1854, the United States and Japan signed a treaty of trade, peace, and friendship. The treaty opened Japanese harbors to American ships.

U.S. Navy Commodore Matthew C. Perry sailed into a Japanese harbor with four warships in 1853. This show of power and strength helped open trade between the United States and Japan.

The Japanese government spent a lot of money to make their businesses, schools, and army more modern. People in Japan were charged high taxes to pay for these changes. Many people left Japan because they could not pay the taxes.

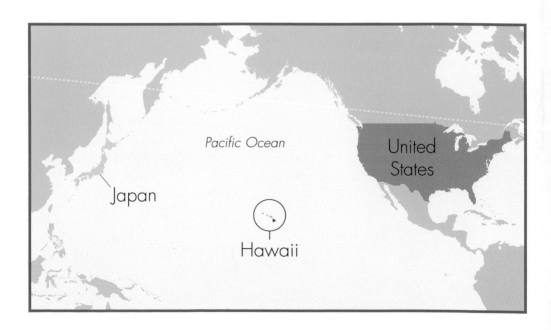

Pacific Ocean

United States

Japan

Hawaii

Early Immigrants

In 1885, the first large group of Japanese immigrants came to Hawaii. Many came to work on sugarcane or pineapple plantations. After working for a few years, some of these immigrants returned to Japan. Others stayed in Hawaii and started their own businesses.

Hawaiian pineapple plantation

Hawaiian sugarcane plantation

By 1899, about 26,000 Japanese had come to
Hawaii. Many Japanese immigrants agreed to work
for three years in Hawaii, for about $15 a month.
That's the same as about $315 a month today.

In Hawaii, Japanese workers were often treated badly by the plantation owners. If workers missed a day of work because of sickness, they had to work two extra days to make it up. Workers were often whipped for working too slowly or fined for being late to work.

Most Japanese immigrants were single men. They planned to make money and then return to their families in Japan. However, many could not save enough to return to Japan.

Coming to the Mainland

The journey from Japan to the United States took about 15 to 28 days on a ship. Japanese immigrants were crowded into small areas on the ships. They often had very little food to eat.

From 1885 to 1924, about 180,000 Japanese immigrants came to the U.S. mainland. Most of them went to Angel Island, in California, where they waited in a camp. While they waited, the U.S. government decided whether or not they would be allowed to stay in the country.

Angel Island, San Francisco Bay, California

Life in America

In America, many Japanese immigrants found jobs as farmworkers. Others became railroad workers and miners.

Early Japanese immigrants were not allowed to become U.S. citizens or to own land. Many immigrants traveled from farm to farm, stopping to pick the different crops. Others started their own small farms by renting land or buying it in the names of their children, who were U.S. citizens.

By the 1920s, most Japanese immigrants lived along the west coast of the United States in California. Many Americans did not like the Japanese because of their skin color and how they looked. In 1924, the United States changed their laws to stop all immigration from Japan.

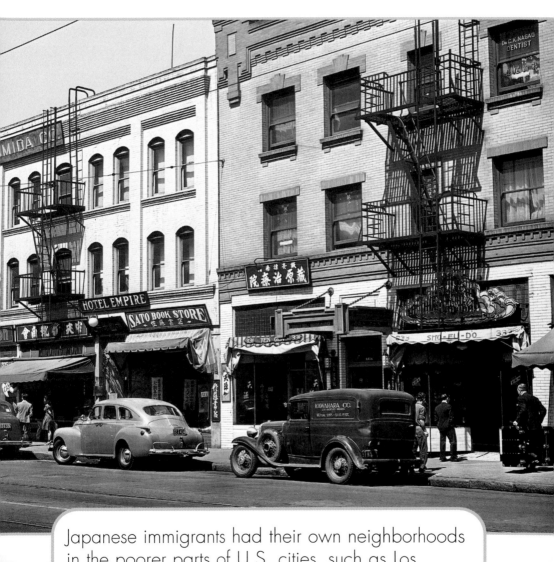

Japanese immigrants had their own neighborhoods in the poorer parts of U.S. cities, such as Los Angeles, California. These neighborhoods were called Japantowns or Little Tokyos.

After Japan attacked Pearl Harbor, Hawaii, in 1941, the United States entered World War II. The U.S. government feared that some Japanese Americans might help Japan during the war. Starting in 1942, many Japanese Americans were forced to live in camps where they stayed until the end of the war.

Buses took Japanese Americans from their homes to camps.

During World War II, about 120,000 Japanese were held in guarded camps in the United States. More than half of them were children and young adults. Entire families were often crowded into one room.

When World War II ended in 1945, the Japanese people living in the camps were freed. However, many Japanese immigrants had lost their homes, property, and businesses while they were in the camps. It wasn't until 1952 that the Japanese were allowed to become U.S. citizens.

Many Japanese American women served in the U.S. Army during World War II.

During World War II, about 33,000 Japanese Americans served in the U.S. armed forces. These American soldiers received more than 18,000 medals for bravery —more than any other military group in United States history.

The Fact Box

In 1988, the U.S. government gave $20,000 to every Japanese American who had been in a camp during World War II.

Japanese Immigrants Today

There are about 796,000 Japanese Americans today. Japanese Americans have worked hard to help the United States grow. They have added much to the American way of life.

Japanese immigrants have introduced other Americans to foods, such as sushi and teriyaki, as well as to the Japanese sport of karate.

Many Japanese Americans have started successful businesses in the United States. Gilroy, California, is known as the Garlic Capital of the World because Kiyoshi Hirasaki, a Japanese American, was once the largest producer of garlic in California.

Yoko Ono is a Japanese immigrant who has become a successful artist and businesswoman in America. She was married to John Lennon of the Beatles.

Glossary

attacked (uh-**takd**) to have tried to hurt someone
or something

citizens (**siht**-uh-zuhnz) natives of a country who have
the right to live there

commodore (**kah**-muh-dohr) a captain in the United
States Navy

immigrant (**ihm**-uh-gruhnt) a person who comes into a
country to live there

mainland (**mayn**-land) the largest land of a country that
does not include the islands

plantations (plan-**tay**-shuhnz) large farms where only
one crop is grown

property (**prahp**-uhr-tee) something that belongs
to a person

territory (**tehr**-uh-tohr-ee) the land and waters that are
controlled by a country or state

treaty (**tree**-tee) an official understanding, signed and
agreed upon by two or more countries

World War II (**werld wor too**) war fought mainly in
Europe, Asia, and Africa from 1939 to 1945

Resources

Books

Japanese Immigrants, 1850–1950
by Rosemary Wallner
Blue Earth Books (2001)

*I Am an American: A True Story
of Japanese Internment*
by Jerry Stanley
Crown Publishing (1996)

Web Sites

Due to the changing nature of Internet links, PowerKids Press has developed an online list of Web sites related to the subjects of this book. This site is updated regularly. Please use this link to access the list:

http://www.powerkidslinks.com/cta/jap/

Index

Word Count: 422

Note to Librarians, Teachers, and Parents

If reading is a challenge, Reading Power is a solution! Reading Power is perfect for readers who want high-interest subject matter at an accessible reading level. These fact-filled, photo-illustrated books are designed for readers who want straightforward vocabulary, engaging topics, and a manageable reading experience. With clear picture/text correspondence, leveled Reading Power books put the reader in charge. Now readers have the power to get the information they want and the skills they need in a user-friendly format.